MUFFINS AND BREADS

Bounty
BOOKS

Introduction

There's something so very comforting about a batch of muffins fresh from the oven, or a loaf of home-baked bread. Time to take baking a step further with some wonderful new recipes for scones, tea loaves and buns from around the world. We guarantee these tempting treats will disappear before they even have chance to cool on the rack!

ACP Magazines Ltd and Bounty Books hereby exclude all liability to the extent permitted by law for any errors or omissions in this book and for any loss, damage or expense (whether direct or indirect) suffered by a third party relying on any information contained in this book.

This paperback edition published in 2011 by Bounty Books, a division of Octopus Publishing Group Limited, Endeavour House, 189 Shaftesbury Avenue, London WC2H 8JY www.octopusbooks.co.uk

An Hachette UK Company www.hachette.co.uk

Reprinted 2011, 2012

ISBN: 978-0-753722-07-7

Printed and bound in China

contents

muffins
sweet & savoury

Muffins are simple to make and delicious eaten hot, warm or cold, with or without butter. They are best made on the day of serving. All of our mouth-watering recipes will make either 12 medium or 6 large muffins.

Evenly greased muffin trays should be slightly more than half-filled with mixture

To test if muffins are cooked, push a skewer into a muffin; when withdrawn, the skewer should be free from muffin mixture

NOTE These recipes have not been tested to cook in a microwave oven.

▪ We used a medium-sized muffin tray (80ml capacity), and a larger muffin tray (180ml capacity). Other sized trays are available, but you will need to adjust baking times if you use these trays. Trays should be slightly more than half-filled with mixture, whatever size you use. Trays should be greased evenly or coated with non-stick spray.

▪ Butter should be firm from the refrigerator when it is to be chopped.

▪ Muffin mixtures require minimum mixing and should look coarse and lumpy. We found a large metal spoon or fork to be the best implement for mixing.

▪ Muffins are cooked when they are browned, risen, firm to touch and beginning to shrink from the sides of the pan. If in doubt, push a metal or wooden skewer into a muffin. When withdrawn, the skewer should be clean and free from muffin mixture. Turn muffins from the tray onto a wire rack as soon as they are baked to prevent them from becoming steamy. However, if muffins have a filling such as custard, caramel or jam, let them stand a few minutes before turning them onto a wire rack. These fillings can be extremely hot, so handle them carefully.

▪ Cold muffins freeze well; transfer to freezer wrap or freezer bags before freezing. Press bag gently or use a freezer pump to expel all the air. Correctly wrapped muffins can be frozen for up to 3 months.

▪ To thaw in a conventional oven, remove freezer wrap and re-wrap muffins individually in foil, place in a single layer on an oven tray in a moderate oven for about 20 minutes or until they reach the right eating temperature for you.

▪ Microwave ovens vary in power, so we can give only a general guide to thawing muffins this way. Remove freezer wrap from muffins, place in a single layer in the oven. Set the oven to DEFROST, MEDIUM LOW or 30%, according to your oven. Allow about 45 seconds for 1 muffin; 1 minute for 2 muffins; and 1½ minutes for 4 muffins. Stand muffins for 10 to 15 seconds. Thawed muffins should not feel hot to the touch. If they feel hot, they are over-heated. You may need to experiment for best results.

the basic muffin recipe
– easy as one, two, three...

PREPARATION TIME 10 MINUTES BAKING TIME 20 MINUTES

375g SELF-RAISING FLOUR
90g BUTTER, CHOPPED
220g CASTER SUGAR
310ml BUTTERMILK
1 EGG, LIGHTLY BEATEN

1 Grease 12 hole (80ml capacity) muffin tray. Sift flour into large bowl, rub in butter.
2 Stir in sugar, buttermilk and egg. Do not over-mix; mixture should be lumpy.
3 Spoon mixture into prepared tray, bake in moderately hot oven 20 minutes.

MAKES 12

SIMPLE VARIATIONS

fruit & spice

3 TEASPOONS MIXED SPICE
190g MIXED DRIED FRUIT

Sift spice with flour; add fruit with sugar.

date & orange

160g WHOLEMEAL SELF-RAISING FLOUR
240g STONED CHOPPED DATES
3 TEASPOONS GRATED ORANGE RIND

Substitute the wholemeal self-raising flour for 150g of the self-raising flour in basic muffin recipe. Add dates and rind with sugar.

choc chip & walnut

140g CHOCOLATE CHIPS
120g CHOPPED WALNUTS

opposite page: date & orange; fruit & spice (top tier) basic; choc chip & walnut (bottom tier)

Add chocolate chips and nuts with sugar.

blueberry muffins

PREPARATION TIME 10 MINUTES BAKING TIME 20 MINUTES

300g SELF-RAISING FLOUR
150g FIRMLY PACKED BROWN
SUGAR
150g FRESH OR FROZEN
BLUEBERRIES
1 EGG, LIGHTLY BEATEN
180ml BUTTERMILK
125ml VEGETABLE OIL

1 Grease 6 hole (180ml capacity) muffin tray.
2 Sift dry ingredients into large bowl, stir in remaining ingredients.
3 Spoon mixture into prepared tray. Bake in moderately hot oven about 20 minutes.

MAKES 6

banana date muffins

PREPARATION TIME 10 MINUTES BAKING TIME 20 MINUTES

300g SELF-RAISING FLOUR
1 TEASPOON MIXED SPICE
100g FIRMLY PACKED BROWN
SUGAR
2 LARGE (460g) BANANAS, MASHED
160g STONED CHOPPED DATES
3 EGGS, LIGHTLY BEATEN
80ml VEGETABLE OIL
80ml BUTTERMILK

1 Grease 12 hole (80ml capacity) muffin tray.
2 Sift dry ingredients into large bowl, stir in remaining ingredients.
3 Spoon mixture into prepared tray. Bake in moderately hot oven about 20 minutes.

MAKES 12

day-before muffins

PREPARATION TIME 15 MINUTES (PLUS REFRIGERATION TIME)
COOKING TIME 30 MINUTES

100g COARSELY CHOPPED DRIED APRICOTS
95g COARSELY CHOPPED DRIED FIGS
95g ALL-BRAN BREAKFAST CEREAL
375ml SKIMMED MILK
250g FIRMLY PACKED BROWN SUGAR
1½ TABLESPOONS GOLDEN SYRUP
185g SELF-RAISING FLOUR
60g PECANS, CHOPPED COARSELY

1   Combine apricot, fig, cereal, milk, sugar and syrup in large bowl; mix well. Cover; refrigerate overnight.
2   Preheat oven to moderately hot. Lightly grease four holes only of a six-hole large 180ml muffin tray.
3   Stir flour and nuts into apricot mixture. Spoon mixture into prepared muffin tray; bake in moderately hot oven 30 minutes. Serve muffins hot or cold. Dust with sifted icing sugar and top with dried apricots, if desired.

SERVES 4

■ If you like to eat your muffins with butter, create your own complementary flavoured butter. Bring butter to room temperature and beat in a small quantity of the flavouring – try crushed berries, jam, honey or maple syrup. Crush some honeycomb with a rolling pin and fold into the softened butter. For a savoury alternative, use baked garlic (wrap unpeeled garlic clove in foil and bake in a moderate oven until the garlic softens and can be squeezed from the clove; mash with butter), or try finely chopped mixed herbs, olives, roasted peppers or anchovies.

TIP Muffins can be frozen for up to 2 months.

rhubarb crumble muffins

375g SELF-RAISING FLOUR
130g FIRMLY PACKED BROWN
SUGAR
100g BUTTER, MELTED
250ml MILK
1 EGG, LIGHTLY BEATEN

FILLING
190g CHOPPED FRESH RHUBARB
55g CASTER SUGAR
2 TABLESPOONS WATER
1/4 TEASPOON GRATED LEMON RIND

CRUMBLE TOPPING
35g PLAIN FLOUR
65g FIRMLY PACKED BROWN SUGAR
2 TABLESPOONS TOASTED MUESLI
1 TEASPOON GRATED LEMON RIND
30g BUTTER, MELTED

PREPARATION TIME 20 MINUTES BAKING TIME 20 MINUTES

1 Grease 12 hole (80ml capacity) muffin tray.
2 Sift dry ingredients into large bowl, stir in remaining ingredients.
3 Half-fill prepared tray with muffin mixture, spoon filling into wells, top with remaining muffin mixture, spread carefully to cover filling. Sprinkle with crumble topping, press gently onto muffin mixture. Bake in moderately hot oven about 20 minutes.

FILLING Combine all ingredients in small pan, bring to boil, simmer, uncovered, 5 minutes or until mixture is thick and rhubarb soft; cool.

CRUMBLE TOPPING Combine all ingredients in small bowl; mix well.

MAKES 12

choc brownie muffins

PREPARATION TIME 10 MINUTES BAKING TIME 20 MINUTES

300g SELF-RAISING FLOUR
35g COCOA POWDER
75g CASTER SUGAR
60g BUTTER, MELTED
95g CHOCOLATE CHIPS
75g CHOPPED PISTACHIOS
125ml NUTELLA
1 EGG, LIGHTLY BEATEN
180ml MILK
125ml SOURED CREAM

1 Grease 12 hole (80ml capacity) muffin tray.
2 Sift dry ingredients into large bowl, stir in remaining ingredients.
3 Spoon mixture into prepared tray. Bake in moderately hot oven about 20 minutes.

MAKES 12

citrus poppy seed muffins

PREPARATION TIME 15 MINUTES BAKING TIME 20 MINUTES

125g SOFT BUTTER
2 TEASPOONS GRATED LEMON RIND
2 TEASPOONS GRATED LIME RIND
2 TEASPOONS GRATED ORANGE RIND
150g CASTER SUGAR
2 EGGS
300g SELF-RAISING FLOUR
125ml MILK
2 TABLESPOONS POPPY SEEDS

1 Grease 12 hole (80ml capacity) muffin tray.
2 Place butter, rinds, sugar, eggs, sifted flour and milk in medium bowl, beat with electric mixer until just combined, then beat on medium speed until mixture is just changed in colour; stir in poppy seeds.
3 Spoon mixture into prepared tray. Bake in moderately hot oven about 20 minutes.

MAKES 12

marmalade almond muffins

300g SELF-RAISING FLOUR
125g BUTTER, CHOPPED
80g FLAKED ALMONDS
150g CASTER SUGAR
1 TABLESPOON GRATED ORANGE
RIND
125ml ORANGE MARMALADE
2 EGGS, LIGHTLY BEATEN
125ml MILK
20g FLAKED ALMONDS, EXTRA

PREPARATION TIME 10 MINUTES BAKING TIME 20 MINUTES

1 Grease 12 hole (80ml capacity) muffin tray.
2 Stir flour into large bowl, rub in butter. Stir in nuts, sugar and rind, then marmalade, eggs and milk.
3 Spoon mixture into prepared tray, sprinkle with extra nuts. Bake in moderately hot oven about 20 minutes.

MAKES 12

asparagus, salmon & mustard muffins

200g FRESH ASPARAGUS
375g SELF-RAISING FLOUR
2 EGGS, LIGHTLY BEATEN
250ml BUTTERMILK
2 TABLESPOONS DIJON MUSTARD
125g BUTTER, MELTED
100g SMOKED SALMON, FINELY CHOPPED

TOPPING
30g BUTTER
40g CHOPPED ALMONDS
1 TABLESPOON FINELY GRATED PARMESAN CHEESE
1 TEASPOON DRAINED GREEN PEPPERCORNS, CRUSHED

1   Grease 12 hole (80ml capacity) muffin tray. Snap off and discard tough ends of asparagus. Boil, steam or microwave asparagus until just tender. Drain, rinse under cold water, drain on kitchen paper; cool. Chop asparagus roughly.
2   Sift flour into large bowl, stir in eggs, buttermilk, mustard and butter, then asparagus and salmon.
3   Spoon mixture into prepared tray, sprinkle with topping. Bake in moderately hot oven about 20 minutes.

TOPPING   Melt butter in small pan, add nuts, stir over heat until just beginning to brown. Stir in cheese and peppercorns.

MAKES 12

■ Savoury muffins make great snacks and should be quite strong in flavour. Season the mixtures with salt and pepper to make sure they taste good after they're baked. Try muffins as an accompaniment to soup, with casseroles or, as an alternative, with a robust salad for a light supper.

■ To prepare asparagus: using vegetable peeler, scrape away the large nodules from stem, leaving the small nodules intact near tip. Bend each spear of asparagus near the coarse end. You will feel a spot where spear will snap. Break away coarse, woody end and discard it.

chickpea & spinach muffins

PREPARATION TIME 20 MINUTES **BAKING TIME** 25 MINUTES

40g CORNMEAL
1 TABLESPOON VEGETABLE OIL
4 SPRING ONIONS, CHOPPED
2 CLOVES GARLIC, CRUSHED
40 SPINACH LEAVES, SHREDDED
300g SELF-RAISING FLOUR
170g CORNMEAL, EXTRA
2 TABLESPOONS FINELY CHOPPED
FRESH BASIL LEAVES
1 EGG, LIGHTLY BEATEN
310ml MILK
90g BUTTER, MELTED
300g CAN CHICKPEAS, RINSED,
DRAINED
2 TABLESPOONS FINELY GRATED
PARMESAN CHEESE

1   Grease 6 hole (180ml capacity) muffin tray. Sprinkle inside of trays with about half the cornmeal. Heat oil in medium pan, add onion and garlic, cook, stirring, until onion is just soft. Add spinach, cook, stirring, until spinach is just wilted; cool.
2   Sift flour and extra cornmeal into large bowl, stir in basil, egg, milk and butter, then spinach mixture and chickpeas.
3   Spoon mixture into prepared tray, sprinkle with cheese and remaining cornmeal. Bake in moderately hot oven about 25 minutes.

MAKES 6

prosciutto, basil & tomato muffins

PREPARATION TIME 15 MINUTES   BAKING TIME 30 MINUTES

5 SLICES (75g) PROSCIUTTO
375g SELF-RAISING FLOUR
90g BUTTER
1 EGG, LIGHTLY BEATEN
310ml BUTTERMILK
80ml MILK
50g DRAINED CHOPPED SUN-DRIED
TOMATOES
2 TABLESPOONS CHOPPED FRESH
BASIL LEAVES
1 CLOVE GARLIC, CRUSHED
1 TEASPOON CRACKED BLACK
PEPPER
1 TABLESPOON OLIVE OIL

1   Grease 6 hole (180ml capacity) muffin tray. Cut prosciutto into strips.
2   Sift flour into large bowl, rub in butter, stir in egg, buttermilk, milk, tomatoes, basil, garlic and pepper.
3   Spoon mixture into prepared tray, top with prosciutto, brush lightly with oil. Bake in moderately hot oven about 20 minutes. Cover with foil, bake a further 10 minutes.

MAKES 6

TIP Use bottled pesto to save time. A sun-dried tomato pesto can also be used.

mini muffin dampers

PREPARATION TIME 10 MINUTES BAKING TIME 25 MINUTES

450g SELF-RAISING FLOUR
40g BUTTER, CHOPPED COARSELY
430ml BUTTERMILK
2 TABLESPOONS BASIL PESTO
90g COARSELY GRATED CHEDDAR CHEESE
1/4 TEASPOON SWEET PAPRIKA
1 TABLESPOON PLAIN FLOUR

1 Preheat oven to moderately hot. Grease 12-hole 80ml muffin tray.
2 Place self-raising flour in large bowl; rub in butter with fingertips. Using fork, stir in buttermilk to form a soft, sticky dough. Swirl pesto and cheese through; do not overmix.
3 Divide mixture among holes of prepared tray. Sprinkle with combined paprika and plain flour.
4 Bake in moderately hot oven 25 minutes.
5 Stand dampers in tray 5 minutes before turning out onto wire rack.

MAKES 12

■ Buttermilk is sold alongside fresh milk products in supermarkets. A good lower-fat substitute for dairy products such as cream or sour cream, it is good in baking and salad dressings and makes the texture of these muffins particularly delicious. Serve the muffins warm as a snack or make tiny one-bite muffins in mini muffin pans and serve them as finger food.

Scones served hot from the oven with butter or jam and cream are delightful for morning or afternoon tea. Often, cooks are judged by the scones they can make. There is no mystery about making light, fluffy scones; you must make a soft, sticky dough and the dough should be kneaded quickly and lightly. The rest is up to the oven; it should be very hot to make the scones rise quickly.

ingredients

FLOUR If you like the taste and texture of wholemeal, try using half white self-raising flour and half wholemeal self-raising flour instead of all white flour; you will need a little more liquid to make the dough soft and sticky. The amount of liquid needed to achieve a soft, sticky dough depends on the way the flour absorbs the liquid; this depends on the quality and age of the flour.

SUGAR A little sugar added to a scone dough takes away the floury taste; you can use any type of sugar you like; raw, brown, white or even icing sugar.

LIQUID The liquid added to scones can be varied. You can use cream or any type of milk, including buttermilk. Commercial sour cream, light sour cream or plain yogurt can be used too, but will need to be broken down with some water to achieve a similar consistency to milk. Water can be used by itself, giving you a very pale scone. Water and milk or any of the above-mentioned dairy products can be mixed together for the liquid.

BUTTER Butter is an optional extra in scones; it adds a little flavour and colour to the cooked scones.

SALT We haven't added salt to our recipe, but, if you like, a pinch of salt can be added to the flour.

handling the dough

Scone dough should be patted out flat using hand. A rolling pin is useful if making large quantities of dough. Don't roll dough heavily or too thinly.

cutters

We like to use sharp metal cutters for scones; they don't squash the dough, but simply cut through it.

scone cooking tips

■ We like to cook scones in a cake tin with sides about 3cm (1in) or 4cm (1½in) high. This gives the scones a 'wall' to stop them toppling over, and it also allows them to brown evenly on top.

■ Don't squash the scones into the tin; they should be just touching. They will expand as well as rise, and over-crowding makes it difficult to cook scones in the middle.

■ It is important to cook scones at a very high temperature. Experiment with your oven to find the shelf position and temperature that give you the best results.

■ As a guide, the hottest part of the oven gives the best results for scones. This varies depending on the type of oven, the way the heat is distributed and the type of fuel used by the oven. Always check oven manufacturers' instructions.

■ The scones in the middle of the tin will take the longest time to cook. After the cooking time has expired, tap the centre scones firmly with your fingertips; scones should sound hollow and look evenly browned.

■ Turn scones onto wire rack. For soft scones, wrap immediately in clean tea-towel or table napkin; for scones with crisp tops, leave on the rack to cool, uncovered.

basic scones

PREPARATION TIME 20 MINUTES BAKING TIME 15 MINUTES

375g SELF-RAISING FLOUR
1 TABLESPOON CASTER SUGAR
1/4 TEASPOON SALT
30g BUTTER
180ml MILK
125ml WATER, APPROXIMATELY

1 Grease a 23cm (9in) square shallow cake tin. Sift flour, sugar and salt into large bowl, rub in butter with fingertips.
2 Using a knife, stir in milk and enough water to make a sticky dough.
3 Turn dough onto floured surface, knead quickly and lightly until smooth.
4 Use hand to press dough out evenly to 2cm (¾in) thickness, cut into 5cm (2in) rounds. Gently knead scraps of dough together, and repeat pressing and cutting out of dough. Place rounds in prepared tin; brush with a little extra milk, if desired. Bake in very hot oven about 15 minutes.

SIMPLE VARIATIONS

lemon & currant

1 QUANTITY BASIC SCONE RECIPE
75g CURRANTS
2 TEASPOONS GRATED LEMON RIND

Add currants and rind to flour mixture. Proceed as for basic scone method.

cumin seed & oregano

1 QUANTITY BASIC SCONE RECIPE
2 TABLESPOONS CHOPPED FRESH OREGANO
3 TEASPOONS CUMIN SEEDS
2 TEASPOONS GROUND CUMIN
1 TABLESPOON TOMATO PASTE

Add oregano and cumin to flour mixture. Proceed as for basic scone method, adding tomato paste with milk.

apricot wholemeal

75g CHOPPED DRIED APRICOTS
125ml BOILING WATER
225g WHITE SELF-RAISING FLOUR
160g WHOLEMEAL SELF-RAISING FLOUR
1 TABLESPOON CASTER SUGAR
1/4 TEASPOON SALT
30g BUTTER
180ml MILK, APPROXIMATELY

Place dried apricots in small heatproof bowl, pour over boiling water, let stand for 15 minutes or until cool. Proceed as for basic scone method. After butter is rubbed into the flour, add undrained apricot mixture along with enough milk to mix to a soft, sticky dough.

opposite page: basic scones, lemon and currant, apricot wholemeal, cumin seed and oregano (clockwise from top right)

glazed apricot & almond scones

PREPARATION TIME 20 MINUTES   BAKING TIME 15 MINUTES

450g SELF-RAISING FLOUR
1 TEASPOON MIXED SPICE
2 TEASPOONS CASTER SUGAR
30g BUTTER
150g DRIED APRICOTS, CHOPPED
45g ROUGHLY CHOPPED SLIVERED
ALMONDS, TOASTED
1 EGG, LIGHTLY BEATEN
310ml MILK, APPROXIMATELY
2 TABLESPOONS SIEVED
APRICOT JAM

1   Grease 23cm (9in) square shallow baking tin. Sift flour, spice and sugar into large bowl, rub in butter. Add apricots and nuts, stir in egg and enough milk to mix to a soft, sticky dough.
2   Turn dough onto floured surface, knead until smooth. Press dough out to 3cm (1in) thickness, cut into 5.5cm (2¼in) rounds, place into prepared tin.
3   Bake in hot oven about 15 minutes, brush with jam.

MAKES 16

carrot banana scones

300g WHITE SELF-RAISING FLOUR
80g WHOLEMEAL SELF-RAISING FLOUR
1/2 TEASPOON GROUND CARDAMOM
40g BUTTER
65g FIRMLY PACKED BROWN SUGAR
1 LARGE (230g) BANANA, MASHED
1 MEDIUM (120g) CARROT, FINELY GRATED
30g FINELY CHOPPED WALNUTS
40g FINELY CHOPPED RAISINS
180ml MILK, APPROXIMATELY

ORANGE CREAM
50g PACKAGED CREAM CHEESE, CHOPPED
50g BUTTER, CHOPPED
1/2 TEASPOON GRATED ORANGE RIND
80g ICING SUGAR

1   Grease 23cm (9in) round sandwich cake tin. Sift flours and cardamom into large bowl, rub in butter. Add sugar, banana, carrot, nuts and raisins, stir in enough milk to mix to a soft, sticky dough.
2   Turn dough onto floured surface, knead until smooth. Press dough out to 2cm (¾in) thickness, cut into 5.5cm (2¼in) rounds, place into prepared tin.
3   Bake in very hot oven about 20 minutes. Serve with orange cream.

ORANGE CREAM Beat cheese, butter and rind in small bowl with electric mixer until as white as possible. Gradually beat in sifted icing sugar.

MAKES 12

scones: sweet & savoury

spicy fruit scones

PREPARATION TIME 20 MINUTES
(PLUS STANDING TIME)
BAKING TIME 15 MINUTES

310ml HOT STRONG BLACK TEA,
STRAINED
135g MIXED DRIED FRUIT
450g SELF-RAISING FLOUR
1 TEASPOON GROUND CINNAMON
1 TEASPOON MIXED SPICE
2 TABLESPOONS CASTER SUGAR
20g BUTTER
125ml SOURED CREAM,
APPROXIMATELY

1 Grease 23cm (9in) square
shallow baking tin. Combine tea
and fruit in small heatproof bowl,
cover, stand 20 minutes or until
mixture has cooled.
2 Sift dry ingredients into large
bowl, rub in butter. Stir in fruit
mixture and enough soured
cream to mix to a soft, sticky
dough.
3 Turn dough onto floured
surface, knead until smooth.
Press dough out to 2cm (¾in)
thickness, cut into 5.5cm (2¼in)
rounds, place into prepared tin.
4 Bake in hot oven about
15 minutes.

MAKES 16

honey wholemeal scones

PREPARATION TIME 20 MINUTES
BAKING TIME 20 MINUTES

300g WHITE SELF-RAISING FLOUR
160g WHOLEMEAL SELF-RAISING FLOUR
½ TEASPOON GROUND CINNAMON
20g BUTTER
60ml HONEY
250ml MILK, APPROXIMATELY

1 Grease 19cm x 29cm (7½in x 11½in) rectangular shallow baking tin. Sift dry ingredients into medium bowl, rub in butter, stir in honey and enough milk to mix to a soft, sticky dough.
2 Turn dough onto floured surface, knead until smooth. Press dough out to 2cm (¾in) thickness, cut into 5.5cm (2¼in) rounds, place into prepared tin.
3 Bake in hot oven about 20 minutes.

MAKES 15

TIP You will need to cook about 250g pumpkin for this recipe. Recipe best made just before serving.

Don't worry if the butter, sugar and egg mixture curdles.

The amount of milk you need to add to this scone recipe will depend entirely on the water content of the pumpkin – the amount you add will vary every time you make these scones.

pumpkin scones

PREPARATION TIME 20 MINUTES BAKING TIME 15 MINUTES

40g BUTTER
55g CASTER SUGAR
1 EGG, LIGHTLY BEATEN
340g COOKED MASHED PUMPKIN
375g SELF-RAISING FLOUR
1/2 TEASPOON GROUND NUTMEG
85ml MILK, APPROXIMATELY

1 Lightly grease two 20cm (8in) round sandwich tins.
2 Beat butter and sugar in small bowl with electric mixer until light and fluffy; gradually beat in egg. Transfer mixture to large bowl.
3 Stir in pumpkin, then sifted dry ingredients and enough milk to make a soft sticky dough. Turn dough onto floured surface, knead lightly until smooth.
4 Press dough out to about 2cm (¾in) in thickness, cut 5cm (2in) rounds from dough. Place rounds, just touching, in prepared tins. Brush tops with a little milk.
5 Bake scones in very hot oven about 15 minutes.

MAKES ABOUT 16

blueberry ginger scones with custard cream

PREPARATION TIME 20 MINUTES BAKING TIME 15 MINUTES

300g SELF-RAISING FLOUR
3 TEASPOONS GROUND GINGER
55g CASTER SUGAR
50g BUTTER
75g FRESH OR FROZEN BLUEBERRIES
60ml SOURED CREAM
125ml MILK, APPROXIMATELY

CUSTARD CREAM
250ml WHIPPING CREAM
125ml THICK CUSTARD
2 TABLESPOONS ICING SUGAR

1 Grease 20cm (8in) round sandwich cake tin. Sift flour, ginger and sugar into medium bowl, rub in butter, add berries and sour cream. Stir in enough milk to mix to a soft, sticky dough.
2 Turn dough onto floured surface, knead until smooth. Press dough out to 2cm (¾in) thickness, cut into 5cm (2in) rounds, place into prepared tin.
3 Bake in very hot oven about 15 minutes. Serve scones with custard cream, dusted with sifted icing sugar, if desired.

CUSTARD CREAM Beat cream, custard and sugar in small bowl with electric mixer until soft peaks form.

MAKES 12

scones: sweet & savoury

bacon, egg & mustard scones

PREPARATION TIME 25 MINUTES BAKING TIME 15 MINUTES

2 BACON RASHERS, FINELY CHOPPED
335g SELF-RAISING FLOUR
90g BUTTER, CHOPPED
2 HARD-BOILED EGGS, FINELY CHOPPED
20g FINELY GRATED PARMESAN CHEESE
2 TABLESPOONS CHOPPED FRESH CHIVES
1 TABLESPOON SEEDED MUSTARD
250ml MILK, APPROXIMATELY
2 TABLESPOONS FINELY GRATED PARMESAN CHEESE, EXTRA

1 Grease 23cm (9in) round sandwich cake tin. Cook bacon in pan, stirring, until crisp; drain, cool.
2 Sift flour into medium bowl, rub in butter. Add bacon, eggs, cheese, chives and mustard, stir in enough milk to mix to a soft, sticky dough.
3 Turn dough onto floured surface, knead until smooth. Press dough out to 2cm (¾in) thickness, cut into 5cm (2in) rounds. Place rounds into prepared tin, brush with a little extra milk, sprinkle with extra cheese.
4 Bake in very hot oven about 15 minutes.

MAKES 16

smoked salmon & sour cream scones

300g SELF-RAISING FLOUR
150g SMOKED SALMON,
CHOPPED
4 TABLESPOONS CHOPPED FRESH
DILL TIPS
1/4 TEASPOON GROUND
BLACK PEPPER
80ml SOURED CREAM
250ml BUTTERMILK,
APPROXIMATELY

DILL CREAM
125ml SOURED CREAM
3 TABLESPOONS CHOPPED FRESH
DILL TIPS

PREPARATION TIME 20 MINUTES BAKING TIME 15 MINUTES

1 Grease 19cm x 29cm (7½in x 11½in) rectangular shallow baking tin. Sift flour into medium bowl, stir in salmon, dill and pepper, then soured cream and enough buttermilk to mix to a soft, sticky dough.
2 Turn dough onto floured surface, knead until smooth, press dough out to 2cm (¾in) thickness, cut into 5.5cm (2¼in) rounds, place into prepared tin.
3 Bake in very hot oven about 15 minutes. Serve with dill cream.

DILL CREAM Combine ingredients in small bowl; mix well.

MAKES 12

little crusty cheese & mustard dampers

PREPARATION TIME 20 MINUTES   BAKING TIME 15 MINUTES

600g SELF-RAISING FLOUR
1 TEASPOON DRY MUSTARD
30g BUTTER
500ml MILK, APPROXIMATELY

TOPPING
30g BUTTER
2 TABLESPOONS SEEDED MUSTARD
1/2 TEASPOON CAYENNE PEPPER
120g COARSELY GRATED PARMESAN
CHEESE

1   Sift flour and mustard into large bowl, rub in butter. Stir in enough milk to mix to a soft, sticky dough.

2   Turn dough onto floured surface, knead until smooth. Press dough out to about 1.5cm ($^5/_8$ in) thickness, cut into 7cm (2¾in) rounds. Place rounds, just touching, onto greased baking trays; sprinkle with topping.

3   Bake in hot oven about 15 minutes.

TOPPING Melt butter in small pan, stir in remaining ingredients.

MAKES 14

TIP Use an electric frypan, a frying pan or a solid plate over a griller for cooking drop scones. For best results, turn drop scones just before the bubbles burst.

drop scones

PREPARATION TIME 10 MINUTES   COOKING TIME 20 MINUTES

150g SELF-RAISING FLOUR
55g CASTER SUGAR
PINCH BICARBONATE OF SODA
1 EGG, LIGHTLY BEATEN
185ml MILK, APPROXIMATELY

1   Sift dry ingredients into medium bowl. Make well in centre; gradually stir in egg and enough milk to give a smooth, creamy pouring consistency.
2   Drop dessertspoons of batter from tip of spoon into heated greased frying pan; allow room for spreading. When bubbles begin to appear, turn drop scones; cook until lightly browned on other side. Serve warm with butter or cream and jam.

MAKES ABOUT 15

The drop scone's ancestry is probably the girdle or griddle cake, in which the dough was placed on a hot plate over the fire and quickly baked. There are many variations on the basic recipe; you can substitute wholemeal self-raising flour for half the white self-raising flour; add finely chopped dried fruit, and spices such as cinnamon, ginger, nutmeg and mixed spice add interest. Plain drop scones are usually served with jam and butter or cream.

bread & rolls

All of our delicious breads are made with step-by-step recipes. Some of these recipes use yeast, but even novice cooks shouldn't be deterred from using yeast. It is simply a raising or leavening agent. Baking powder is also used for leavening. Bread with no raising is known as 'unleavened'.

KNEADING Kneading makes the dough smooth, pliable and elastic. Start by scraping the dough from the bowl onto a floured surface in front of you. Now press the heel of one hand gently but firmly into the lump of dough and p-u-u-s-h it away from you. Lift the furthest edge of the dough a little, give the dough a quarter turn, fold the dough in half towards you, and repeat the press-and-push motion. Keep going for the time specified. When kneaded sufficiently, dough will spring back if pressed with a finger.

PROVING An important step is proving the dough, or giving it time to rise after kneading. Place dough in an oiled bowl, turn dough lightly to grease top and prevent a skin forming. Cover bowl with a clean cloth or plastic wrap and stand it in a warm place away from draughts until dough has risen as specified.
■ Refrigerating retards proving. Place the kneaded dough, covered, in the refrigerator for up to 12 hours or until risen as specified.

OVEN HINTS Always check the manufacturer's instructions for your oven. As a guide, the top of the bread should be in the centre of the oven; 220°C is the perfect temperature for baking bread. Sweet breads are baked at slightly lower temperatures. Cover bread loosely with foil if it is overbrowning.
■ To test if bread is cooked, tap bread firmly on the bottom crust with fingers; if it sounds hollow, it is cooked. You will need to turn the bread out of the pan into a tea-towel, tap quickly, and return to the pan for further baking, if necessary. Work with caution, as the bread will be very hot.

NOTE Recipes are unsuitable to microwave. For tips on freezing bread, see page 55.

Working on a floured surface, begin kneading by pressing the heel of one hand gently but firmly into the lump of dough and p-u-u-s-h it away from you

Proving is an important step in the bread-making process; place the kneaded dough in an oiled bowl, cover the bowl and stand it in a warm place until the dough has risen as specified

■ You can use dried yeast or fresh compressed yeast. We use dried yeast packaged in 5 x 7g sachets (2 teaspoons per sachet). Bulk dried yeast is available in 500g or 1kg vacuum-sealed packs; it will keep in a cool, dry place for up to 1 year, if unopened. Store in the refrigerator in an airtight container after opening.

■ Generally, 2 teaspoons (7g) of dried yeast is equivalent to 15g of compressed yeast, but it's a good idea to read and follow the instructions on the packet.

■ Fresh compressed yeast has a limited shelf life and must be stored in the refrigerator in an airtight container.

■ Liquid added to yeast should be warm, about 26°C. An easy 'rule of thumb' method for those without a thermometer is to add $1/3$ boiling liquid to $2/3$ cold. If liquid is too cold, it will retard the yeast growth; if too hot, it will kill the action of the yeast.

■ Gluten is important in bread-making, as it is the protein in flour which gives elasticity to the dough. However, if you are allergic to gluten, try our gluten-free bread.

basic white bread

PREPARATION TIME 25 MINUTES (PLUS STANDING TIME)
BAKING TIME 45 MINUTES

3 TEASPOONS (10g) DRIED YEAST
125ml WARM WATER
2 TEASPOONS SUGAR
375g PLAIN FLOUR
1 TEASPOON SALT
30g BUTTER, MELTED
125ml WARM MILK

1 Combine yeast, water and sugar in small bowl, whisk until yeast dissolves. Cover, stand in warm place about 10 minutes until frothy.
2 Sift flour and salt into large bowl, stir in butter, milk and yeast mixture. Turn dough onto floured surface, knead 10 minutes or until dough is smooth and elastic.
3 Place dough into greased bowl, cover, stand in warm place about 1 hour or until mixture has doubled in size.
4 Turn dough onto floured surface, knead until smooth, roll to 18cm x 35cm (7in x 14in) rectangle, roll up from short side like a Swiss roll, place on greased baking tray, cut 4 diagonal slashes across top. Cover, stand in warm place about 20 minutes or until risen. Bake in moderately hot oven about 45 minutes. Turn bread onto wire rack to cool.

SIMPLE VARIATIONS

brown bread
Substitute the wholemeal plain flour for half the plain flour. You may need to mix in a little more warm milk to make a firm dough.

french sticks
From Step 4: Divide dough in two, shape each into 40cm (16in) sausage, place on 2 greased baking trays, cover, stand in warm place 15 minutes or until dough has risen. Cut slashes on tops, sprinkle with tablespoon of plain flour. Bake in moderately hot oven about 20 minutes.

cottage loaf
Starting at Step 4: Shape dough into 20cm (8in) round, place onto greased oven tray, cover, stand in warm place 15 minutes or until risen. Cut slashes on bread, sprinkle with plain flour. Bake in moderately hot oven 30 minutes.

dinner rolls
Starting at Step 4: Divide dough into 12 portions, shape into rolls, place onto greased baking trays, cover, stand in warm place 15 minutes or until risen. Cut slashes on rolls, brush with milk, sprinkle with seeds, if desired. Bake in moderately hot oven about 20 minutes.

opposite page: basic white bread loaf, cottage loaf, brown bread, french sticks, dinner rolls (clockwise from bottom left)

baps

2 TEASPOONS (7g) DRIED YEAST
1 TEASPOON SUGAR
125ml WARM WATER
125ml WARM MILK
335g PLAIN FLOUR
1 TEASPOON SALT
40g BUTTER

PREPARATION TIME 20 MINUTES (PLUS STANDING TIME)
BAKING TIME 15 MINUTES

1   Combine yeast, sugar, water and milk in small bowl, whisk until yeast is dissolved. Cover bowl, stand in warm place about 10 minutes or until mixture is frothy.

2   Sift flour and salt into large bowl, rub in butter. Stir in yeast mixture, mix to a soft dough. Turn dough onto floured surface, knead about 5 minutes or until smooth and elastic. Place dough in a large greased bowl, cover, stand in warm place about 1 hour or until dough has doubled in size.

3   Turn dough onto floured surface, knead until smooth, divide dough into 6 equal portions, knead into balls. Place balls about 5cm (2in) apart on floured baking tray. Dust lightly with a little extra sifted flour, cover with cloth. Stand in warm place about 10 minutes or until dough is well risen.

4   Dust balls again with a little more sifted flour, indent centres with a finger. Bake in hot oven about 15 minutes.

MAKES 6

gluten-free bread

PREPARATION TIME 10 MINUTES
BAKING TIME 1 HOUR (PLUS STANDING TIME)

450g GLUTEN-FREE PLAIN FLOUR
180g BUCKWHEAT FLOUR
2 TEASPOONS GLUTEN-FREE BAKING POWDER
1½ TEASPOONS SALT
160g SUNFLOWER SEED KERNELS
70g BUTTER, CHOPPED
375ml MILK
2 EGGS, LIGHTLY BEATEN
2 TEASPOONS POPPY SEEDS

1 Sift flours, baking powder and salt into large bowl; stir in kernels.
2 Rub in butter; stir in combined milk and eggs; do not overmix.
3 Press mixture into greased 14cm x 21cm (5½in x 8¼in) loaf
tin; do not smooth top. Brush with a little extra milk, sprinkle with
seeds. Bake in moderate oven about 1 hour. Stand bread 10 minutes
before turning onto wire rack to cool.

MAKES 1 LOAF

mixed grain loaf

50g CRACKED BUCKWHEAT
80g BULGAR WHEAT
50g KIBBLED RYE
3 TEASPOONS (10g) DRIED YEAST
1 TEASPOON SUGAR
180ml WARM MILK
60ml WARM WATER
335g WHITE PLAIN FLOUR
80g WHOLEMEAL PLAIN FLOUR
1 TEASPOON SALT
1 TABLESPOON LINSEEDS
2 TEASPOONS OLIVE OIL
1 EGG YOLK
1 TEASPOON MILK, EXTRA
2 TEASPOONS SESAME SEEDS
2 TEASPOONS CRACKED BUCKWHEAT, EXTRA

bread & rolls

1 Place buckwheat, bulgar wheat and kibbled rye in small heatproof bowl, cover with boiling water, cover, stand 30 minutes. Rinse well, drain well.

2 Combine yeast, sugar, milk and water in small bowl, whisk until yeast is dissolved. Cover, stand in warm place about 10 minutes or until mixture is frothy. Sift flours and salt into large bowl, add grain mixture and linseeds. Stir in oil and yeast mixture; mix to a soft dough. Turn dough onto floured surface, knead about 10 minutes or until dough is smooth and elastic. Place dough in large greased bowl, cover, stand in warm place about 1 hour or until dough has doubled in size.

3 Turn dough onto floured surface, knead until smooth. Divide dough into 3 pieces. Shape each piece into a 30cm (12in) sausage. Plait sausages, place into greased 14cm x 21cm (5½in x 8¼in) loaf tin. Cover, stand in warm place about 30 minutes or until risen.

4 Brush dough with combined egg yolk and extra milk, sprinkle evenly with combined sesame seeds and extra buckwheat. Bake in moderately hot oven about 45 minutes.

MAKES 1 LOAF

greek easter bread

2 TEASPOONS (7g) DRIED YEAST
1 TEASPOON CASTER SUGAR
180ml WARM MILK
75g PLAIN FLOUR
100g BUTTER, MELTED
2 EGGS, LIGHTLY BEATEN
75g CASTER SUGAR, EXTRA
450g PLAIN FLOUR, EXTRA
2 TEASPOONS GROUND ANISEED
1/2 TEASPOON SALT
1 EGG YOLK
2 TABLESPOONS MILK, EXTRA

PREPARATION TIME 25 MINUTES (PLUS STANDING TIME)
BAKING TIME 40 MINUTES

1 Combine yeast, sugar and milk in large bowl, whisk until yeast is dissolved. Whisk in sifted flour, cover, stand in warm place about 45 minutes or until mixture has doubled in size. Whisk in butter, eggs and extra sugar. Stir in sifted extra flour, aniseed and salt in 2 batches. Turn dough onto floured surface, knead about 10 minutes or until smooth. Place dough in large greased bowl, cover, stand in warm place about 1½ hours or until dough has doubled in size.

2 Turn dough onto floured surface, knead until smooth. Divide dough into 6 portions. Shape each portion into a 33cm (13in) sausage. Twist 2 sausages together; shape into a round. Repeat with remaining sausages. Place the 3 rounds close together on a lightly greased baking tray, brush joins with water, press rounds gently together.

2 Cover rounds, stand in warm place about 45 minutes or until risen. Brush rounds with combined yolk and extra milk, bake in moderately hot oven 10 minutes, reduce heat to moderate, bake about a further 30 minutes.

MAKES 1 LOAF

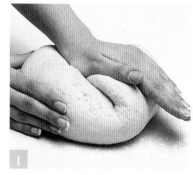

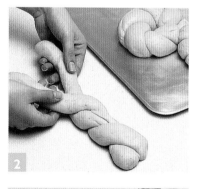

irish soda bread

PREPARATION TIME 15 MINUTES
BAKING TIME 50 MINUTES

420g WHOLEMEAL PLAIN FLOUR
375g WHITE PLAIN FLOUR
1 TEASPOON SALT
1 TEASPOON BICARBONATE OF SODA
680ml BUTTERMILK, APPROXIMATELY

1 Sift flours, salt and soda into large bowl. Stir in enough buttermilk
to mix to a firm dough.
2 Turn dough onto floured surface, knead until just smooth. Shape
dough into 20 cm (8in) round, place on greased baking tray.
3 Cut 1cm (½in) deep slashes in round in a cross shape, brush with
a little milk. Bake in moderate oven about 50 minutes. Lift onto wire
rack to cool.

MAKES 1 LOAF

pumpernickel bread

PREPARATION TIME 25 MINUTES (PLUS STANDING TIME) BAKING TIME 45 MINUTES

2 TEASPOONS (7g) DRIED YEAST
1 TEASPOON SUGAR
250ml WARM WATER
50g BUTTER, MELTED
1 TABLESPOON MOLASSES
1 TABLESPOON CARAWAY SEEDS
85g CORNMEAL
185g RYE FLOUR
150g PLAIN FLOUR
2 TABLESPOONS COCOA POWDER
1 TEASPOON SALT

This bread, originating in Westphalian Germany, is a dense, dark bread. Here the bread is made with rye flour and yeast, although it can also be made with a sourdough starter. The sourdough acts as the rising agent to leaven the dough. This is known as the sourdough method and dates back to the earliest known breads made in Egypt around 4000BC.

1   Combine yeast, sugar and water in large bowl, whisk until yeast is dissolved; cover, stand in warm place about 10 minutes or until mixture is frothy. Stir in butter and molasses, then seeds, cornmeal and sifted flours, cocoa and salt. Turn dough onto floured surface, knead about 10 minutes or until smooth.

2   Place dough into greased bowl, cover, stand in warm place about 2 hours or until dough has doubled in size.

3   Grease 8cm x 26cm (3¼in x 10¼in) shallow cake tin, line sides of tin with 2 layers of baking paper, extending 5cm (2in) above edge of tin. Turn dough onto floured surface, knead until smooth. Press dough into prepared tin. Cover loosely, stand in warm place about 45 minutes or until dough has risen to top of tin.

4   Cover pan with a sheet of foil. Bake in moderate oven 15 minutes, remove foil, bake about a further 30 minutes.

MAKES 1 LOAF

onion focaccia

PREPARATION TIME 20 MINUTES
(PLUS STANDING TIME)
BAKING TIME 25 MINUTES

300g PLAIN FLOUR
½ TEASPOON SALT
2 TEASPOONS (7g) DRIED YEAST
20g GRATED PARMESAN CHEESE
1 TABLESPOON CHOPPED FRESH
ROSEMARY
1 TABLESPOON CHOPPED FRESH
SAGE LEAVES
2 TEASPOONS CHOPPED FRESH PARSLEY
2 TABLESPOONS OLIVE OIL
250ml WARM WATER
1 SMALL (80g) ONION, FINELY SLICED
1 TABLESPOON SEA SALT
1 TABLESPOON OLIVE OIL, EXTRA

1 Sift flour and salt into large bowl,
stir in yeast, cheese and herbs. Pour in
oil and water, gradually stir in flour;
mix to a soft dough.
2 Turn dough onto floured surface,
knead about 5 minutes or until dough
is smooth and elastic.
3 Place dough on greased oven tray,
press into 24cm (9½in) round. Cover
dough with greased cling film, stand
in warm place about 1 hour or until
doubled in size.
4 Remove cling film. Sprinkle dough
with sliced onion and sea salt, drizzle
with extra oil. Bake in hot oven
about 25 minutes. Lift onto wire rack
to cool.

MAKES 1 LOAF

chilli corn bread

PREPARATION TIME 10 MINUTES   BAKING TIME 1 HOUR

150g SELF-RAISING FLOUR
1 TEASPOON SALT
170g CORNMEAL
100g KIBBLED RYE
1 TABLESPOON BROWN SUGAR
1 TEASPOON GROUND CUMIN
2 TABLESPOONS CHOPPED FRESH PARSLEY
1 TEASPOON CHOPPED FRESH THYME
60g GRATED CHEDDAR CHEESE
310g CAN CREAMED CORN
90g FROZEN CORN KERNELS, THAWED
160ml BUTTERMILK
80ml MILK
2 TEASPOONS SAMBAL OELEK
2 EGGS, LIGHTLY BEATEN
50g BUTTER, MELTED

1   Grease deep 19cm (7½in) square cake tin, line base with baking parchment. Sift flour and salt into large bowl, stir in cornmeal, rye, sugar, cumin, herbs and cheese.
2   Combine remaining ingredients in medium bowl; mix well, stir into dry ingredients.
3   Spread mixture into prepared tin, bake in moderately hot oven about 1 hour. Stand, covered, 10 minutes before turning onto wire rack to cool.

MAKES 1 LOAF

bread & rolls

bagels

PREPARATION TIME 20 MINUTES (PLUS STANDING TIME) BAKING TIME 20 MINUTES

3 TEASPOONS (10g) DRIED YEAST
1 TABLESPOON CASTER SUGAR
125ml WARM WATER
250ml WARM MILK
450g PLAIN FLOUR
3 TEASPOONS SALT
1 TABLESPOON CASTER SUGAR, EXTRA
1 EGG YOLK
1 TEASPOON WATER, EXTRA
1 TABLESPOON POPPY SEEDS
2 TEASPOONS SEA SALT

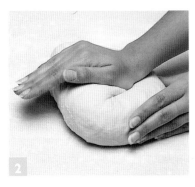

1   Combine yeast, sugar, water and milk in large bowl, whisk until yeast is dissolved. Cover bowl, stand in warm place about 10 minutes or until mixture is frothy. Stir sifted flour, salt and extra sugar into yeast mixture in 2 batches; mix to a firm dough.

2   Turn dough onto floured surface, knead about 10 minutes or until dough is smooth and elastic. Place dough into large greased bowl, cover, stand in warm place about 1 hour or until dough has doubled in size.

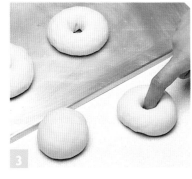

3   Turn dough onto floured surface, knead until smooth; divide dough into 12 portions. Knead each portion into a ball. Press finger in centre of each ball to make a hole, rotate ball with finger until the hole is one- third the size of the bagel. Place bagels about 3cm (1in) apart on greased oven trays, cover, stand in warm place about 15 minutes, or until risen.

4   Drop bagels individually into pan of boiling water; they must not touch. Turn bagels after 1 minute, boil further minute, remove with slotted spoon. Place bagels on greased baking trays. Brush tops with combined egg yolk and extra water, sprinkle with combined seeds and sea salt. Bake in moderately hot oven about 20 minutes. Cool on wire rack.

MAKES 12

■ It is believed that bagels originated in the Jewish communities of eastern Europe and were introduced to America by immigrants. To create your own favourite, try flavouring with cinnamon, onion, currants, blueberries and rye flour. The classic filling for plain bagels is cream cheese and smoked salmon topped with capers.

STORAGE Breadsticks can be kept in an airtight container 2 weeks.

cheese breadsticks

PREPARATION TIME 30 MINUTES (PLUS STANDING TIME)
BAKING TIME 10 MINUTES

60g BUTTER, MELTED
1 TEASPOON DRIED YEAST
2 TABLESPOONS OLIVE OIL
2 TEASPOONS SUGAR
½ TEASPOON SALT
100g GRATED PARMESAN CHEESE
180ml WARM WATER
375g PLAIN FLOUR

1   Combine butter, yeast, oil, sugar, salt, cheese and the water in large bowl; gradually stir in flour. Knead on lightly floured surface about 10 minutes or until smooth and elastic. Place dough in large oiled bowl; turn to coat in oil. Stand in warm place 10 minutes.
2   Cut dough into quarters; roll each part into 10 logs, about 20cm (8in) long. Place 1cm (½in) apart on lightly greased baking trays.
3   Bake, uncovered, in hot oven about 20 minutes or until crisp and browned; cool on wire racks.

MAKES 40

olive bread with oregano

PREPARATION TIME 25 MINUTES (PLUS STANDING TIME)
BAKING TIME 45 MINUTES

1 TABLESPOON DRIED YEAST
1 TEASPOON SUGAR
560ml SKIMMED MILK
825g PLAIN FLOUR
80ml OLIVE OIL
150g PITTED BLACK OLIVES, HALVED
2 TABLESPOONS COARSELY
CHOPPED FRESH OREGANO
2 TABLESPOONS PLAIN FLOUR,
EXTRA

1   Combine yeast, sugar and milk in large bowl; stir in 450g of the flour. Cover; stand in warm place 30 minutes or until foamy. Stir in oil, then remaining flour. Knead on floured surface about 10 minutes or until smooth and elastic. Place dough in large oiled bowl. Cover; stand in warm place until doubled in size.

2   Meanwhile, drain olives on kitchen paper.

3   Turn dough onto floured surface; knead in olives and oregano. Roll dough into 30cm x 35cm (11¾in x 13¾in) oval; fold almost in half. Place on large greased baking tray; sift 2 tablespoons of plain flour over dough.

4   Bake, uncovered, in moderately hot oven 45 minutes or until cooked when tested; cool on wire rack.

SERVES 10

STORAGE Bread can be made a day ahead and warmed before serving. Store in airtight container.

farmhouse spinach & double cheese plait

PREPARATION TIME 20 MINUTES BAKING TIME 40 MINUTES

500g SPINACH
15g BUTTER
1 MEDIUM (350g) LEEK, FINELY CHOPPED
2 TEASPOONS CHOPPED FRESH THYME
300g SELF-RAISING FLOUR
80g FINELY GRATED PARMESAN CHEESE
1 TEASPOON SEASONED PEPPER
3 TABLESPOONS CHOPPED FRESH BASIL LEAVES
150g FETA CHEESE, CRUMBLED
250ml MILK, APPROXIMATELY

1 Add spinach to pan of boiling water, boil 1 minute, drain, rinse under cold water; drain well. Squeeze excess moisture from spinach, chop finely.

2 Heat butter in pan, add leek and thyme, cook, stirring occasionally, until leek is soft. Add spinach, cook, stirring, about 5 minutes or until any liquid has evaporated; cool.

3 Sift flour into medium bowl, stir in parmesan, pepper, basil, three-quarters of the feta cheese, spinach mixture and enough milk to mix to a soft, sticky dough.

4 Turn dough onto floured surface, knead until smooth. Divide dough into 3 pieces, shape into 36cm (14in) sausages. Plait sausages together on greased baking tray, sprinkle with remaining feta cheese.

5 Bake in moderately hot oven about 40 minutes.

MAKES 1 LOAF

TIPS ON FREEZING BREAD

▪ Large unbaked loaves are not satisfactory to freeze at home.

▪ Small breads such as dinner rolls, pizza bases and unglazed sweet buns are suitable to freeze if partly baked. Follow the recipe, but bake for only half the time, cool on the oven tray, then freeze, uncovered, on the tray until firm. Transfer to freezer wrap or freezer bags before storing in the freezer; press bag gently or use a freezer pump to expel all the air. Such products can be frozen for up to 3 months.

▪ To complete baking, thaw completely at room temperature and continue baking as specified in the recipe.

▪ To freeze baked loaves, cool bread as quickly as possible, pack in good-quality freezer bags, expel all air, and freeze as quickly as possible. It can be a good idea to slice the bread first so that you can take out just the amount you want. Correctly wrapped bread can be frozen for up to 3 months.

cheese & olive loaf

OLIVES A staple of Mediterranean cuisines, olives are used to flavour everything from pizzas to sauces. The olive's flavour and texture is affected by its degree of ripeness when it's picked and the medium in which it is cured – such as brine, salt or oil. Green olives are picked unripe, making them denser in texture and more bitter than brown or black olives, which are left on the tree until fully ripened. Opened cans or jars of olives should be refrigerated, but some olives can be stored at room temperature if they're cured in brine or olive oil.

PREPARATION TIME 15 MINUTES COOKING TIME 35 MINUTES

150g SELF-RAISING FLOUR
50g COARSELY GRATED PARMESAN CHEESE
2 TABLESPOONS COARSELY CHOPPED FRESH MINT
$^1/_2$ TEASPOON GROUND BLACK PEPPER
120g PITTED BLACK OLIVES, CHOPPED COARSELY
75g MORTADELLA, CHOPPED COARSELY
4 EGGS, BEATEN LIGHTLY
80g BUTTER, MELTED

1 Preheat oven to moderately hot. Lightly grease 8cm x 26cm (3¼in x 10¼in) shallow cake tin.
2 Sift flour into medium bowl, add cheese, mint, pepper, olives and mortadella.
3 Add egg and butter; stir until well combined. Spread mixture into tin; bake about 35 minutes or until browned lightly. Turn onto wire rack to cool.

SERVES 6

brioche

PREPARATION TIME 30 MINUTES (PLUS STANDING TIME)
BAKING TIME 25 MINUTES

4 TEASPOONS (14g) DRIED YEAST
80ml WARM WATER
55g CASTER SUGAR
600g PLAIN FLOUR
1 TEASPOON SALT
5 EGGS, LIGHTLY BEATEN
250g BUTTER
1 EGG, LIGHTLY BEATEN, EXTRA
1 TABLESPOON SUGAR

1 Combine yeast, water and 1 tablespoon of the caster sugar in small bowl, whisk until yeast is dissolved. Cover, stand in warm place about 10 minutes or until mixture is frothy. Sift flour, remaining caster sugar and salt into large bowl, add yeast mixture and eggs, stir until just combined. Turn dough onto floured surface, knead about 10 minutes or until dough is smooth and elastic.

2 Divide butter into 10 equal portions, knead each portion into dough, kneading well after each addition until all the butter is incorporated and dough is smooth and glossy. Place dough into large bowl, cover, refrigerate overnight.

3 Divide dough into 3 equal portions, shape into 45cm (18in) sausages. Place sausages onto large greased baking tray, plait sausages, cover, stand in cool place about 1 hour or until dough has nearly doubled in size. Brush plait with extra egg, sprinkle with sugar. Bake in moderately hot oven 10 minutes, reduce heat to moderate, bake a further 15 minutes.

MAKES 1 LOAF

rhubarb ginger damper

PREPARATION TIME 20 MINUTES BAKING TIME 10 MINUTES

15g BUTTER
3 STEMS (200g) RHUBARB, FINELY CHOPPED
300g SELF-RAISING FLOUR
PINCH BICARBONATE OF SODA
1 TEASPOON GROUND CINNAMON
60g GROUND ALMONDS
2 TABLESPOONS FINELY CHOPPED CRYSTALLISED GINGER
75g CASTER SUGAR
250ml MILK, APPROXIMATELY
2 TABLESPOONS CASTER SUGAR, EXTRA

1 Melt butter in small saucepan, add rhubarb, cook, stirring, about 5 minutes or until rhubarb is just tender; cool.
2 Sift flour, soda and cinnamon into medium bowl, stir in nuts, ginger, sugar and rhubarb. Stir in enough milk to mix to a soft, sticky dough.
3 Turn dough onto floured surface, knead until smooth. Divide dough in half, place halves onto greased baking trays, shape into 15cm (6in) rounds. Mark rounds into 8 wedges, sprinkle with extra sugar.
4 Bake in hot oven about 20 minutes.

MAKES 2

panettone

PREPARATION TIME 40 MINUTES (PLUS STANDING TIME)
COOKING TIME 45 MINUTES

85g RAISINS
40g CANDIED MIXED PEEL
80g SULTANAS
80ml SWEET MARSALA
2 TABLESPOONS DRIED YEAST
1 TEASPOON CASTER SUGAR
60ml WARM MILK
750g PLAIN FLOUR
1 TEASPOON SALT
55g CASTER SUGAR, EXTRA
3 EGGS, BEATEN LIGHTLY
3 EGG YOLKS
2 TEASPOONS GRATED ORANGE RIND
1 TEASPOON VANILLA ESSENCE
100g BUTTER, SOFTENED
250ml WARM MILK, EXTRA
1 EGG, BEATEN LIGHTLY, EXTRA

1 Grease two deep 20cm (8in) round cake tins. Using string, tie a collar of greased foil around outside of prepared tins, bringing foil about 6cm (2½in) above edges of tins.
2 Combine fruit with marsala in small bowl. Cover; stand 30 minutes. Combine yeast, sugar and milk in small bowl; whisk until yeast dissolves. Cover bowl; stand in warm place about 10 minutes or until mixture is frothy.
3 Place flour, salt and extra sugar in large bowl; make well in centre. Add eggs and egg yolks, then rind, essence, butter, extra milk, yeast mixture and undrained fruit mixture.
4 Using wooden spoon, beat dough vigorously about 5 minutes (this beating is important). The dough will be soft like cake batter, and will become elastic and leave the side of the bowl. Cover bowl with greased cling film; stand in warm place about 30 minutes or until dough doubles in size. Turn dough onto floured surface; knead about 10 minutes or until smooth. Cut dough in half; knead each half on well-floured surface about 5 minutes or until dough loses its stickiness. Press dough into prepared pans. Cover; stand in warm place about 30 minutes or until dough doubles in size. Brush with extra egg.
5 Bake, uncovered, in moderately hot oven about 15 minutes. Reduce heat to moderate; bake, uncovered, further 30 minutes. Cool on wire racks.

MAKES 2

PANETTONE is an Italian cake made with yeast and containing dried fruit, traditionally eaten at Christmas and Easter. It's traditionally baked in a deep mould to give it height. Panettone can be served as a dessert, accompanied by a sweet wine such as Marsala, and is also delicious toasted and buttered, or, as in this recipe, used in place of bread in a bread and butter pudding.

pineapple macadamia loaf

This is a very quick and easy loaf to make that only involves hand-mixing in one bowl. The recipe contains no butter, but the finished cake is delicious served with lashings of butter.

PREPARATION TIME 15 MINUTES   BAKING TIME 50 MINUTES

450g CAN CRUSHED PINEAPPLE
1 EGG
150g MACADAMIA NUTS, TOASTED, CHOPPED FINELY
150g SELF-RAISING FLOUR
110g CASTER SUGAR
90g DESICCATED COCONUT
125ml MILK

1   Position oven shelves; preheat oven to moderate. Grease 14cm x 21cm (5½in x 8¼in) loaf tin, line base with baking parchment.
2   Drain pineapple, pressing as much syrup as possible from the pineapple; discard syrup.
3   Place pineapple in large bowl, add egg; stir ingredients together with wooden spoon. Stir in remaining ingredients; mix well. Spread mixture into prepared tin.
4   Bake loaf in moderate oven about 50 minutes.
5   Stand loaf 10 minutes, turn onto wire rack, then turn top-side up to cool.

SERVES 20

Toasted macadamia nuts

Pressing syrup from pineapple

Spreading mixture into prepared pan

STORAGE Gingerbread can be made a week ahead. Store in airtight container.

gingerbread

PREPARATION TIME 15 MINUTES (PLUS COOLING TIME)
BAKING TIME 1 HOUR 15 MINUTES

350g GOLDEN SYRUP
250ml WATER
65g FIRMLY PACKED BROWN SUGAR
250g BUTTER
525g PLAIN FLOUR
1 TEASPOON BICARBONATE OF SODA
2 TABLESPOONS GROUND GINGER
1 TEASPOON GROUND NUTMEG
1 TEASPOON GROUND CINNAMON

LEMON ICING
60g BUTTER, SOFTENED
2 TEASPOONS GRATED LEMON RIND
2 TABLESPOONS LEMON JUICE
320g ICING SUGAR

GINGER, which is native to Asia, was first used in Western Europe more than 2000 years ago. Gingerbread is thought to be one of the world's earliest sweet cakes.

1 Grease 23cm (9in) square shallow cake tin, line base with greased baking parchment;.
2 Combine golden syrup, water, sugar and butter in large pan, stir over heat until butter is melted, bring to boil; remove from heat. Cool to room temperature.
3 Stir sifted dry ingredients into butter mixture in 2 batches, beat gently until smooth.
4 Pour mixture into prepared tin; bake in moderately slow oven about 1¼ hours. Stand for 5 minutes before turning onto wire rack to cool. Spread cold gingerbread with lemon icing.

LEMON ICING Beat butter and rind in small bowl with wooden spoon, gradually beat in juice and sifted icing sugar.

SERVES 16

date & walnut rolls

180g CHOPPED DATES
60g BUTTER
100g BROWN SUGAR, FIRMLY
PACKED
250ml WATER
1/2 TEASPOON BICARBONATE
OF SODA
1 EGG, LIGHTLY BEATEN
50g CHOPPED WALNUTS
300g SELF-RAISING FLOUR

PREPARATION TIME 15 MINUTES (PLUS COOLING TIME)
BAKING TIME 40 MINUTES

1   Grease two 8cm x 17cm (3¼in x 6¾in) roll baking moulds. If you
do not have roll moulds, use a similar size loaf tin.
2   Combine dates, butter, sugar and water in saucepan; stir over
heat, without boiling, until sugar is dissolved. Bring to boil, remove
from heat; cool.
3   Stir soda, egg, nuts and sifted flour into date mixture.
4   Spoon mixture evenly into prepared moulds, replace lids.
Bake, standing upright, in moderate oven about 40 minutes. Stand
rolls 10 minutes before removing lids and turning onto wire rack
to cool. Serve sliced with butter.

MAKES 2 ROLLS

TIPS Only ever half fill the
roll moulds with mixture.
Be careful of hot steam when
turning out the cooked rolls.

STORAGE Loaf can be
made 2 days ahead. Store
in airtight container.

fruit & nut loaf

20 MINUTES (PLUS STANDING TIME)
40 MINUTES

2 TEASPOONS (7g) DRIED YEAST
55g CASTER SUGAR
2 TABLESPOONS WARM WATER
160ml WARM MILK
150g PLAIN FLOUR
I EGG, LIGHTLY BEATEN
2 TEASPOONS GRATED ORANGE RIND
300g PLAIN FLOUR, EXTRA
I TEASPOON SALT
$\frac{1}{2}$ TEASPOON GROUND CINNAMON
100g BUTTER, SOFTENED
40g SULTANAS
40g RAISINS
35g CURRANTS
30g CHOPPED WALNUTS, TOASTED
I EGG YOLK
I TABLESPOON CASTER SUGAR, EXTRA
$\frac{1}{2}$ TEASPOON GROUND CINNAMON, EXTRA

1 Grease 14cm x 21cm (5½in x 8¼in) loaf tin, line base with baking parchment. Combine yeast, 2 teaspoons of the sugar and water in large bowl, whisk until yeast is dissolved. Whisk in milk and sifted flour. Cover, stand in warm place about 30 minutes or until mixture is frothy.

2 Stir in egg and rind, then sifted extra flour, salt, cinnamon and remaining sugar. Stir in butter, fruit and nuts.

3 Turn dough onto floured surface, knead until smooth. Place dough into greased bowl, cover, stand in warm place about 1½ hours or until dough has doubled in size.

4 Turn dough onto floured surface, knead until smooth, place into prepared tin. Cover loosely with greased cling film, stand in warm place about 30 minutes or until risen slightly. Remove cling film. Brush dough with egg yolk, sprinkle with combined extra sugar and extra cinnamon. Bake in moderately hot oven 10 minutes, reduce heat to moderate, bake about a further 30 minutes. Turn onto wire rack to cool.

MAKES 1 LOAF

STORAGE This recipe can be made a day ahead and is suitable to freeze.

walnut & raisin loaf

PREPARATION TIME 10 MINUTES BAKING TIME 35 MINUTES

55g RAISINS
90g BUTTER
100g FIRMLY PACKED BROWN SUGAR
80ml WATER
½ TEASPOON BICARBONATE OF SODA
2 EGGS, BEATEN LIGHTLY
60g CHOPPED WALNUTS
75g PLAIN FLOUR
75g SELF-RAISING FLOUR

1 Combine raisins, butter, sugar and the water in medium saucepan; bring to a boil. Remove from heat; stir in soda. Transfer to medium bowl; cool 15 minutes.
2 Preheat oven to slow. Grease 8cm x 25cm (3¼ in x 9¾ in) shallow cake tin; line base with baking parchment.
3 Stir egg and nuts into raisin mixture; stir in sifted flours. Pour mixture into prepared tin. Bake in slow oven about 35 minutes or until cooked when tested by inserting a metal skewer into the loaf. Turn onto wire rack to cool.
4 Serve sliced with brie and grapes.

SERVES 8

olive oil loaf

3 EGGS, BEATEN LIGHTLY
220g CASTER SUGAR
1 TABLESPOON GRATED
ORANGE RIND
335g SELF-RAISING FLOUR
60ml ORANGE JUICE
125ml SKIMMED MILK
250ml EXTRA VIRGIN OLIVE OIL
125ml ORANGE JUICE, WARMED,
EXTRA
40g ICING SUGAR

PREPARATION TIME 25 MINUTES   BAKING TIME 45 MINUTES

1   Oil deep 23cm (9in) square cake tin.
2   Beat egg, sugar and rind in medium bowl with electric mixer
until very thick and creamy and sugar dissolves. Stir in flour, then
combined juice, milk and oil in three batches. Pour mixture into
prepared tin.
3   Bake in moderately hot oven about 45 minutes or until cooked
when tested. Stand loaf in tin 5 minutes; turn onto wire rack placed
over tray. Turn loaf again so it is right-side up.
4   Pour extra juice over hot loaf; sift icing sugar over top of juice.
Cool before serving.

SERVES 10

TIP   Lemon rind and juice
can be substituted for the
orange.

pistachio bread

PREPARATION TIME 10 MINUTES (PLUS STANDING TIME)
BAKING TIME 45 MINUTES

3 EGG WHITES
75g SUGAR
¼ TEASPOON GROUND CARDAMOM
1 TEASPOON FINELY GRATED ORANGE RIND
110g PLAIN FLOUR
110g SHELLED PISTACHIOS

PISTACHIOS are sold in their half-open shells and loose, salted as a snack or unsalted to use in cooking. Their flavour is mild and slightly resinous. Decoratively bright green, they are used to stud pates and terrines, on biscuits, cakes, muffins and confectionery.

1 Preheat oven to moderate. Grease 8cm x 26cm (3¼in x 10¼in) shallow cake tin; line base and sides with baking parchment, extending paper 2cm (¾in) above long sides of tin.
2 Beat egg whites in small bowl with electric mixer until soft peaks form. With motor operating, gradually add sugar, beating until dissolved between additions. Fold in cardamom, rind, flour and nuts; spread bread mixture into prepared tin.
3 Bake in moderate oven about 30 minutes or until browned lightly; cool in tin. Wrap in foil; stand overnight.
4 Preheat oven to low.
5 Using a serrated or electric knife, cut bread on an angle into 3mm slices. Place slices on ungreased baking trays. Bake in low oven about 15 minutes or until dry and crisp; turn onto wire rack to cool.

MAKES 35 SLICES

TIPS Uncut bread can be frozen after the first baking.
    After the second baking, bread slices can be stored up to 4 days in an airtight container.
    For a different spiced version, substitute the cardamom with ½ teaspoon ground cinnamon and 1/4 teaspoon ground nutmeg.

buns
sweet & savoury

fruit & nut scrolls

450g SELF-RAISING FLOUR
2 TEASPOONS CASTER SUGAR
50g BUTTER
330ml BUTTERMILK, APPROXIMATELY

FILLING
40g SULTANAS
35g CURRANTS
35g CHOPPED DRIED APRICOTS
50g CHOPPED STONED PRUNES
1 MEDIUM (150g) APPLE, PEELED,
FINELY CHOPPED
2 TABLESPOONS FLAKED ALMONDS
2 TEASPOONS GRATED ORANGE
RIND
2 TABLESPOONS ORANGE JUICE
$1/3$ TEASPOON GROUND CLOVES
2 TEASPOONS RUM OR BRANDY
50g BROWN SUGAR

APRICOT GLAZE
2 TABLESPOONS APRICOT JAM
2 TEASPOONS WATER

ICING
55g ICING SUGAR
1 TEASPOON HOT WATER

PREPARATION TIME 20 MINUTES   BAKING TIME 15 MINUTES

1   Sift flour and sugar into large bowl, rub in butter. Stir in enough buttermilk to mix to a soft, sticky dough.
2   Turn dough onto floured surface, knead until smooth. Roll dough to 26cm x 36cm (10¼in x 14¼in) rectangle, spread with filling. Roll dough firmly from long side, like a Swiss roll. Cut roll into 2cm (¾in) slices. Place slices, cut side up, about 3cm (1in) apart onto greased baking trays.
3   Bake in very hot oven about 15 minutes. Brush with hot apricot glaze, drizzle with icing.

FILLING Combine all ingredients in medium bowl; mix well.

APRICOT GLAZE Combine jam and water in small pan, simmer few minutes or until glaze thickens slightly; strain.

ICING Combine icing sugar and water in small bowl, stir until smooth, pipe or drizzle over scrolls.

MAKES 18

TIP If you prefer, you can use 380g fruit mincemeat instead of the filling in this recipe.

hot cross buns

Although these delicious Easter treats are now served on Good Friday, in olden times they were thought to have holy powers and were present in many religious observances.

PREPARATION TIME 25 MINUTES (PLUS STANDING TIME)
BAKING TIME 25 MINUTES

4 TEASPOONS (14g) DRIED YEAST
55g CASTER SUGAR
250ml WARM MILK
600g PLAIN FLOUR
1 TEASPOON GROUND CINNAMON
60g BUTTER
1 EGG, LIGHTLY BEATEN
125ml WARM WATER
110g CURRANTS
40g MIXED PEEL
1 TABLESPOON APRICOT JAM

FLOUR PASTE
75g PLAIN FLOUR
1 TABLESPOON CASTER SUGAR
80ml WATER

1   Combine yeast, sugar and milk in small bowl, whisk until yeast is dissolved. Cover bowl, stand in warm place about 10 minutes or until mixture is frothy. Sift flour and cinnamon into large bowl, rub in butter. Stir in yeast mixture, egg, water and fruit, cover, stand in warm place about 1 hour or until mixture has doubled in size.
2   Turn dough onto floured surface, knead about 5 minutes or until smooth and elastic. Divide dough into 16 portions, knead into balls. Place buns into greased 23cm (9in) square shallow cake tin, stand in warm place about 20 minutes or until dough has risen to top of tin.
3   Place flour paste into piping bag fitted with small plain tube, pipe crosses onto buns. Bake in moderately hot oven 10 minutes, reduce heat to moderate, bake about a further 15 minutes. Turn buns onto wire rack, brush with warm sieved jam.

FLOUR PASTE Combine flour and sugar in small bowl, gradually blend in water, stir until smooth.

MAKES 16

buns: sweet & savoury

caramel apple pull-apart

300g SELF-RAISING FLOUR
30g BUTTER
250ml MILK, APPROXIMATELY
65g FIRMLY PACKED BROWN
SUGAR
410g CAN PIE APPLES
PINCH GROUND NUTMEG
½ TEASPOON GROUND
CINNAMON
30g CHOPPED PECANS, TOASTED

CARAMEL
60ml CREAM
20g BUTTER
100g FIRMLY PACKED BROWN
SUGAR

PREPARATION TIME 20 MINUTES BAKING TIME 25 MINUTES

1 Grease deep 22cm (9in) round cake tin. Sift flour into medium
bowl, rub in butter, stir in enough milk to mix to a soft, sticky dough.
2 Turn dough onto floured surface, knead until smooth. Roll dough
onto floured baking paper to 21cm x 40cm (8¼in x 16in) rectangle. Sprinkle dough with sugar, spread with combined apples and
spices to within 3cm (1in) from long edge. Using paper as a guide,
roll dough up like a Swiss roll. Use a floured, serrated knife to cut
roll into 12 slices. Place 11 slices upright around edge of tin; place
remaining slice in centre.
3 Bake pull-apart in moderately hot oven about 25 minutes. Stand
a few minutes before turning onto wire rack to cool. Brush hot
pull-apart evenly with caramel, sprinkle with nuts.

CARAMEL Combine all ingredients in small pan, stir constantly over
heat, without boiling, until sugar is dissolved. Simmer, uncovered,
without stirring, about 3 minutes or until mixture is thickened slightly.

MAKES 1

buns: sweet & savoury

butterscotch curls

A rich butterscotch mixture of brown sugar, butter and nuts makes a simple scone dough special.

60g BUTTER
65g BROWN SUGAR
25g CHOPPED WALNUTS
450g SELF-RAISING FLOUR
90g BUTTER, EXTRA
310ml MILK, APPROXIMATELY
65g BROWN SUGAR, EXTRA

TIP Curls are best eaten hot, split and with butter.

STORAGE Curls can be prepared 3 hours ahead; covered, at room temperature. Uncooked curls are suitable for freezing.

PREPARATION TIME 20 MINUTES BAKING TIME 25 MINUTES

1 Grease deep 20cm (8in) round cake tin. Beat butter and sugar together in small bowl with wooden spoon until just combined, spread over base of prepared tin; sprinkle with nuts.
2 Sift flour into bowl, rub in half the extra butter. Add enough milk to mix to a firm dough. Knead gently on floured surface until smooth. Roll dough to 23cm x 28cm (9in x 11in) rectangle.
3 Melt remaining extra butter, brush over dough, sprinkle with extra sugar. Roll up as for Swiss roll, from long side. Cut into 10 rounds, place cut-side up in prepared tin.
4 Bake in moderately hot oven about 25 minutes.

MAKES 10

buns: sweet & savoury

chelsea buns

When the London suburb of Chelsea was a village in the country, fashionable people, even royalty, would gather at the Chelsea Bun House to enjoy its delicious fare.

4 TEASPOONS (14g) DRIED YEAST
1 TEASPOON CASTER SUGAR
560g PLAIN FLOUR
375ml WARM MILK
1/2 TEASPOON GROUND CINNAMON
1/4 TEASPOON GROUND NUTMEG
1/2 TEASPOON MIXED SPICE
2 TEASPOONS GRATED ORANGE RIND
1 TABLESPOON CASTER SUGAR, EXTRA
1 EGG, LIGHTLY BEATEN
45g BUTTER, MELTED
15g BUTTER, MELTED, EXTRA
2 TABLESPOONS RASPBERRY JAM
75g CURRANTS
50g BROWN SUGAR
60g CHOPPED PECANS, TOASTED
3 TEASPOONS HONEY

COFFEE ICING
240g ICING SUGAR
15g BUTTER, MELTED
2 TABLESPOONS WARM MILK
3 TEASPOONS COFFEE POWDER

1 Combine yeast, caster sugar, 1 tablespoon of the flour and milk in small bowl, whisk until yeast is dissolved. Cover, stand in warm place about 10 minutes or until mixture is frothy. Combine remaining sifted flour, spices, rind and extra caster sugar in large bowl, stir in egg, butter and yeast mixture; mix to a soft dough. Turn dough onto floured surface, knead about 10 minutes or until elastic. Place dough in large greased bowl, cover, stand in warm place about 1 hour or until doubled in size.

2 Turn dough onto floured surface, knead 1 minute. Roll to a 23cm x 36cm (9in x 14¼in) rectangle. Brush dough with extra butter, spread with jam. Sprinkle with combined currants, brown sugar and nuts, leaving a 2cm (¾in) border.

3 Roll dough up from long side, like a Swiss roll. Cut into 12 slices. Place slices, cut side up, in 2 greased 22cm (9in) round cake tins. Cover, stand in warm place about 30 minutes or until dough has risen slightly. Bake in moderately hot oven 30 minutes. Cool buns in tin 10 minutes, transfer to wire rack. Brush hot buns with honey, drizzle with coffee icing.

COFFEE ICING Sift icing sugar into small bowl, stir in butter, milk and coffee, stir until smooth.

MAKES 2

pizza buns

300g SELF-RAISING FLOUR
15g BUTTER
180ml MILK, APPROXIMATELY
2 TEASPOONS OLIVE OIL
1 TABLESPOON CHOPPED FRESH
THYME
2 TEASPOONS PACKAGED
BREADCRUMBS

FILLING
2 TEASPOONS OLIVE OIL
1/2 SMALL (40g) ONION, FINELY
CHOPPED
3 BACON RASHERS, FINELY CHOPPED
1 CLOVE GARLIC, CRUSHED
60g MUSHROOMS, FINELY CHOPPED
3 PITTED BLACK OLIVES, FINELY
CHOPPED
1 TABLESPOON TOMATO PASTE
1 TABLESPOON CHOPPED FRESH
THYME

PREPARATION TIME 20 MINUTES   BAKING TIME 30 MINUTES

1   Grease 20cm (8in) ring cake tin. Sift flour into medium bowl, rub in butter, stir in enough milk to mix to a soft, sticky dough.
2   Turn dough onto floured surface, knead until smooth. Divide dough into 8 pieces, knead each piece until smooth, press each piece to 10cm (4in) round, fill with a teaspoon of filling, pinch edges together to seal, shape into balls. Place balls into prepared tin. Brush with oil, sprinkle with combined thyme and breadcrumbs.
3   Bake in very hot oven 10 minutes, reduce heat to moderately hot, bake about a further 20 minutes.

FILLING Heat oil in saucepan, add onion, bacon and garlic, cook, stirring, until bacon is crisp. Stir in mushrooms, olives, paste and thyme; cool.

MAKES 8

Rolling out the dough into ovals

Sprinkling the tops of the buns with cheese and bacon

cheese & bacon buns

PREPARATION TIME 20 MINUTES (PLUS STANDING TIME)
BAKING TIME 20 MINUTES

4 TEASPOONS (14g) DRIED YEAST
1 TEASPOON SUGAR
375ml WARM WATER
750g PLAIN FLOUR
2 TEASPOONS SALT
125ml MILK
2 TABLESPOONS SUGAR, EXTRA
60g BUTTER, MELTED
1 EGG, LIGHTLY BEATEN
1 TABLESPOON MILK, EXTRA
155g GRATED CHEDDAR CHEESE
4 BACON RASHERS, FINELY
CHOPPED

1　Combine yeast, sugar and water in small bowl, whisk until yeast is dissolved. Cover bowl, stand in warm place about 10 minutes or until mixture is frothy.
2　Sift flour and salt into large bowl. Stir in yeast mixture, milk, extra sugar and butter; mix to a soft dough. Knead on floured surface about 5 minutes or until elastic. Place dough in greased bowl, cover; stand in warm place or until dough has risen.
3　Turn dough onto floured surface, knead until smooth. Divide dough into 16 portions, roll each to a 10cm x 12cm (4in x 5in) oval. Place onto greased baking trays, cover with greased cling film, stand in warm place about 15 minutes or until dough has risen.
4　Remove cling film. Brush rolls with combined egg and extra milk, sprinkle evenly with cheese and bacon. Bake in moderately hot oven about 20 minutes.

MAKES 16

cheesy coriander pesto knots

PREPARATION TIME 25 MINUTES BAKING TIME 15 MINUTES

335g SELF-RAISING FLOUR
2 TEASPOONS CASTER SUGAR
1/4 TEASPOON SALT
30g BUTTER
250ml MILK, APPROXIMATELY
100g HARD GOAT'S CHEESE
GROUND BLACK PEPPER

PESTO
40g FIRMLY PACKED FRESH CORIANDER LEAVES
40g COARSELY GRATED PARMESAN CHEESE
80g PINE NUTS, TOASTED
1 CLOVE GARLIC, CRUSHED
2 TABLESPOONS OLIVE OIL
1 TABLESPOON WATER

PESTO originates from Liguria in Italy, where it is traditionally served with linguine, green beans and boiled new potatoes. Its very versatile consistency and delicious flavour have made it a perfect ingredient to carry across into a host of other dishes.

1 Sift flour, sugar and salt into medium bowl, rub in butter. Stir in enough milk to mix to a soft, sticky dough.
2 Turn dough onto floured surface, knead until smooth. Roll dough into a 17cm x 30cm (6¾in x 11¾in) rectangle. Spread dough with pesto, top with crumbled cheese; sprinkle with pepper. Cut dough crossways into 3cm (1in) strips. Hold both ends of a dough strip in each hand, loop dough as if to make a knot; tuck ends under neatly. Place knots on greased baking trays about 2cm (¾in) apart.
3 Bake in very hot oven about 15 minutes.

PESTO Process coriander, cheese, nuts and garlic until combined. With motor operating, gradually add oil in a thin stream; add water, process until smooth.

MAKES 10

desserts

summer pudding

Summer pudding is commonly made using stale bread; we've developed our own version with a twist, using homemade sponge cake but, of course, you can use bread if you prefer.

3 EGGS
110g CASTER SUGAR
1 TABLESPOON CORNFLOUR
110g SELF-RAISING FLOUR
1 TEASPOON BUTTER
60ml BOILING WATER
75g CASTER SUGAR, EXTRA
125ml WATER
300g FROZEN BLACKBERRIES
500g FROZEN MIXED BERRIES
80g BLACKBERRY JAM

PREPARATION TIME 30 MINUTES (PLUS REFRIGERATION TIME)
COOKING TIME 25 MINUTES

1 Preheat oven to moderate. Grease 25cm x 30cm (9¾in x 11¾in) Swiss roll tin; line base with baking parchment, extending paper 5cm (2in) over long sides.
2 Beat eggs in small bowl with electric mixer until thick and creamy. Gradually add sugar, beating until sugar dissolves; transfer mixture to large bowl.
3 Fold triple-sifted flours into egg mixture. Pour combined butter and boiling water down side of bowl; fold into egg mixture. Spread mixture into tin; bake 15 minutes. Cool in tin.
4 Meanwhile, combine extra sugar and the water in medium saucepan; bring to a boil. Stir in berries; return to a boil. Reduce heat; simmer, uncovered, until berries soften. Strain over medium bowl; reserve syrup and berries separately.
5 Turn cake onto board. Line 1.25-litre pudding basin with plastic wrap, extending wrap 10cm (4in) over side of basin. Cut circle slightly smaller than top edge of basin from cake using tip of sharp knife; cut second circle exact size of base of basin from cake. Cut remaining cake into 10cm (4in) long strips.
6 Place small cake circle in base of basin and use cake strips to line side of basin. Pour 165ml of the reserved syrup into small jug; reserve. Fill basin with berries; cover with remaining syrup, top with large cake circle. Cover pudding with overhanging cling film, weight pudding with saucer; refrigerate 3 hours or overnight.
7 Stir jam and two tablespoons of the reserved syrup in small saucepan until heated through. Turn pudding onto serving plate; brush with remaining reserved syrup then jam mixture. Serve with whipped cream, if desired.

SERVES 6

college pudding

PREPARATION TIME 15 MINUTES   COOKING TIME 1 HOUR
30 MINUTES

80g JAM
125g BUTTER
1 TEASPOON VANILLA ESSENCE
110g CASTER SUGAR
2 EGGS
300g SELF-RAISING FLOUR
125ml MILK

1   Grease aluminium pudding basin (2-litre capacity). Spoon jam into base of pudding basin.

2   Beat butter, essence and sugar in small bowl with electric mixer until light and fluffy. Beat in eggs one at a time, beating well until combined. Transfer mixture to large bowl; stir in sifted flour and milk in two batches.

3   Spread mixture into pudding basin, cover with greased foil, secure with string or lid. Place pudding basin in large pan with enough boiling water to come halfway up side of basin; boil, covered, about 1½ hours or until firm. Replenish water as necessary.

4   Serve with custard, cream or ice-cream.

SERVES 6 TO 8

TIP Use the jam of your choice in this delicious steamed pudding.

STORAGE Recipe best made just before serving.

desserts

Recipe can be made a day ahead; store in an airtight container. Babas can be frozen without syrup.

15g COMPRESSED YEAST
40g PLAIN FLOUR
65g WARM MILK
115g PLAIN FLOUR, EXTRA
2 TABLESPOONS CASTER SUGAR
2 EGGS, LIGHTLY BEATEN
60g BUTTER, MELTED

RUM SYRUP
330g CASTER SUGAR
250ml WATER
2 TABLESPOONS DARK RUM

rum baba

PREPARATION TIME 25 MINUTES (PLUS STANDING TIME)
COOKING TIME 15 MINUTES

1 Grease 6 moulds (125ml capacity).
2 Cream yeast with flour and milk in small bowl; cover; stand in warm place about 10 minutes or until mixture is frothy.
3 Sift extra flour and sugar into large bowl, stir in yeast mixture, eggs and butter; beat about 3 minutes with wooden spoon until batter is smooth. Place batter in large greased bowl, cover; stand in warm place about 40 minutes or until batter has doubled in size.
4 Beat batter again. Divide batter between prepared moulds; stand, uncovered, until batter rises three-quarters of the way up side of moulds. Place moulds on baking tray; bake in moderately hot oven about 15 minutes. Cover tops if beginning to darken too much.
5 Turn babas onto wire rack over tray, pour hot rum syrup over hot babas. Place babas in serving plates; pour syrup from tray over babas until all syrup has been absorbed.

RUM SYRUP Combine sugar and water in pan; stir over heat, without boiling, until sugar is dissolved. Bring to boil; boil, uncovered, without stirring, 2 minutes. Remove from heat, stir in rum.

MAKES 6

RUM BABA It is thought that the earliest version of the rum baba was invented by King Leszczynski of Poland in 1609.

■ Choose either white or dark rum – white is colourless and sweet, used mostly in mixing drinks. For cooking we prefer to use a dark underproof rum (not overproof) for a more subtle flavour.

bread & butter pudding

PREPARATION TIME 20 MINUTES
COOKING TIME 50 MINUTES

1 QUANTITY CUSTARD
6 SLICES WHITE BREAD (270g)
40g BUTTER, SOFTENED
80g SULTANAS
1/4 TEASPOON GROUND NUTMEG

1   Preheat oven to moderately low.
2   Make custard.
3   Grease shallow 2-litre ovenproof dish. Trim crusts from bread. Spread each slice with butter; cut into 4 triangles. Layer bread, overlapping, in dish; sprinkle with sultanas. Pour custard over bread; sprinkle with nutmeg.
4   Place dish in large baking dish; add enough boiling water to come halfway up sides of dish. Bake about 45 minutes or until pudding sets. Remove pudding from baking dish; stand 5 minutes before serving.

SERVES 6

custard

375ml MILK
500ml CREAM
75g CASTER SUGAR
1/2 TEASPOON VANILLA EXTRACT
4 EGGS

Combine milk, cream, sugar and extract in medium saucepan; bring to a boil. Whisk eggs in large bowl; whisking constantly, gradually add hot milk mixture to egg mixture.

STORAGE The puddings on these two pages can be stored, refrigerated, in an airtight container for up to 2 days.

chocolate pecan pudding

PREPARATION TIME 20 MINUTES
COOKING TIME 50 MINUTES

1 QUANTITY CUSTARD
200g CIABATTA, SLICED THICKLY
100g DARK EATING CHOCOLATE, CHOPPED COARSELY
40g COARSELY CHOPPED ROASTED PECANS

1   Preheat oven to moderately low.
2   Grease shallow 2-litre ovenproof dish. Layer bread,
chocolate and nuts, overlapping slices slightly, in dish. Pour
custard over bread.
3   Place dish in large baking dish; add enough boiling water
to come halfway up sides of dish. Bake about 45 minutes or
until pudding sets. Remove pudding from baking dish; stand
5 minutes before serving.

SERVES 6

mincemeat & brioche pudding

PREPARATION TIME 20 MINUTES
COOKING TIME 50 MINUTES

1 QUANTITY CUSTARD
475g JAR MINCEMEAT
2 TABLESPOONS BRANDY
300g BRIOCHE, SLICED THICKLY
1 TABLESPOON DEMERARA SUGAR

1   Preheat oven to moderately low.
2   Combine mincemeat and brandy in small bowl.
3   Grease shallow 2-litre ovenproof dish. Layer bread and
half the fruit mixture, overlapping bread slightly, in dish.
Dollop spoonfuls of remaining fruit mixture over bread.
Pour custard over bread; sprinkle with sugar.
4   Place dish in large baking dish; add enough boiling water
to come halfway up sides of dish. Bake about 45 minutes
or until pudding sets. Remove pudding from baking dish;
stand 5 minutes before serving.

SERVES 6

golden syrup dumplings

PREPARATION TIME 10 MINUTES COOKING TIME 25 MINUTES

185g SELF-RAISING FLOUR
30g BUTTER
115g GOLDEN SYRUP
80ml MILK

SAUCE
30g BUTTER
165g FIRMLY PACKED BROWN SUGAR
175g GOLDEN SYRUP
410ml WATER

1 Sift flour into medium bowl; rub in butter. Gradually stir in golden syrup and milk.
2 Make sauce.
3 Drop rounded tablespoonfuls of mixture into simmering sauce; simmer, covered, about 20 minutes. Serve dumplings with sauce.

SAUCE Combine ingredients in medium saucepan; stir over heat, without boiling, until sugar dissolves. Bring to a boil, without stirring. Reduce heat; simmer, uncovered, 5 minutes.

SERVES 4

GOLDEN SYRUP
is a form of inverted sugar syrup, made in the process of refining sugar cane juice into sugar. This thick, amber-coloured liquid is a staple in many recipes and desserts. It has an appearance not dissimilar to honey, and can also be used as a substitute for corn syrup. Treacle is richer in colour than golden syrup, and has a stronger, slightly bitter flavour.

desserts

glossary

ALL-BRAN a packaged breakfast cereal.

ALMONDS
blanched nuts with skins removed.
flaked sliced nuts.
ground we used packaged commercially-ground nuts.
kernels whole nuts with skins.
slivered nuts cut lengthways.

BAKING POWDER a raising agent consisting mainly of 2 parts cream of tartar to 1 part bicarbonate of soda.

BICARBONATE OF SODA also known as baking soda.

BRIOCHE French in origin; a rich, yeast-leavened, cake-like bread made with butter and eggs. Most common form is the brioche à tête, a round fluted roll topped with a much smaller ball of dough. Available from cake or specialty bread shops.

BULGAR WHEAT hulled, steamed wheat kernels that, once dried, are crushed into various size grains.

BUTTER use salted or unsalted ('sweet') butter; 125g is the equivalent of 1 stick of butter.

BUTTERMILK sold alongside fresh milk products in supermarkets. A good lower-fat substitute for dairy products such as cream or sour cream; good in baking and in salad dressings.

CHEESE
feta a soft Greek cheese with a sharp, salty taste.
goat's made from goat milk; both hard and soft goat cheeses are available.
packaged cream also known as 'Philadelphia'.
parmesan a sharp-tasting hard cheese.
ricotta a fresh, unripened, light curd cheese.
cheddar a mature-tasting, firm-textured cheese.

CHICKPEAS also known as garbanzos; irregularly round, sandy-coloured legumes.

CHOCOLATE
chocolate chips morsels of dark chocolate that hold their shape during baking.
dark we used a good-quality cooking chocolate.
white chips morsels of white chocolate that hold their shape during baking.

COCOA POWDER unsweetened, dried, roasted ground cocoa beans.

COCONUT use desiccated coconut unless otherwise specified.
cream available in cans and cartons.
flaked flaked, dried coconut flesh.
milk pure, unsweetened coconut milk available in cans and cartons.
shredded thin strips of dried coconut.

CORNMEAL ground dried corn (maize); similar to polenta but pale yellow and finer. One can be substituted for the other, but textures will vary.

CRACKED BUCKWHEAT (kasha) crushed buckwheat seeds.

CREAM
fresh (minimum fat content 35%) also known as pure cream and pouring cream; has no additives.
sour (minimum fat content 35%) a thick, commercially cultured soured cream.
whipping (minimum fat content 35%) a cream containing a thickener such as gelatine.

CURRANTS tiny, almost-black raisins, named after a grape variety originating in Corinth, Greece.

CUSTARD POWDER packaged powdered mixture of starch (wheat or corn), artificial flavouring and colouring. Sometimes sold as vanilla pudding mixture.

DATES fruits of the date palm tree, thought to have originated in North Africa, which have a thick, sticky texture and sweet mild flavour. Sometimes sold already pitted and chopped; can be eaten fresh or dried on their own, or cooked to release their flavour.

ESSENCE also known as extract; a flavouring extracted from various plants by distillation.

FLOUR

plain an all-purpose flour, made from wheat.

rye milled from rye grains.

self-raising substitute plain (all-purpose) flour and baking powder in the proportions of 150g plain flour to 2 level teaspoons baking powder. Sift together several times before using.

wholemeal plain a whole-wheat flour without the addition of baking powder.

wholemeal self-raising a wholewheat self-raising flour; add baking powder to wholemeal plain flour as above to make wholemeal self-raising flour.

GOLDEN SYRUP also known as light treacle; a by-product of refined sugarcane. Pure maple syrup or honey can be substituted, but the flavour will vary.

JAM also known as preserve or conserve; most often made from fruit.

KIBBLED RYE cracked rye grains.

MACADAMIAS rich and buttery nuts; store in refrigerator because of high fat content.

MAPLE-FLAVOURED SYRUP made from sugar cane rather than maple-tree sap; used in cooking or as a topping but cannot be considered an exact substitute for pure maple syrup.

MARSALA a sweet fortified wine originally from Sicily.

MILK we used full-cream homogenised milk unless otherwise specified.

sweetened condensed we used canned milk with 60% of the water removed, and the remaining milk sweetened with sugar.

MINCEMEAT a mixture of dried fruits, peel, rind, sugar, alcohol and spices. When cooked, the mixture forms a rich, fruity spread; commonly used as a filling in fruit mince pies.

MIXED FRUIT also known as mixed dried fruit; commonly a combination of sultanas, raisins, currants, mixed peel and cherries. mixed peel also known as candied citrus peel.

MIXED PEEL candied citrus peel.

MIXED SPICE a classic mixture generally containing caraway, allspice, coriander, cumin, nutmeg and ginger, although cinnamon and other spices can be added.

MOLASSES the thick, syrupy end product of raw sugar manufacturing or refining.

MUSTARD

dijon French mustard.

dry powdered mustard seeds.

seeded (or wholegrain) a French-style textured mustard with crushed mustard seeds.

NUTELLA a chocolate hazelnut spread.

OAT BRAN the outer layer of oat grains.

OIL

light olive mild-flavoured olive oil.

olive a blend of refined and virgin olive oils, good for everyday cooking.

vegetable any of a number of oils sourced from plants rather than animal fats; we used a polyunsaturated oil.

PAPRIKA ground dried peppers; flavour varies from mild and sweet to considerably hotter, depending on the variety of pepper.

PECAN native to the United States and now grown locally; golden-brown, buttery and rich in flavour.

PEPPER

black we used both cracked and ground black pepper.

cayenne also known as chilli pepper.

seasoned a combination of black pepper, sugar and capsicum.

PINE NUTS small, cream-coloured soft kernels.

PROSCIUTTO uncooked, unsmoked, cured ham; ready to eat when bought.

PRUNES whole dried plums.

PUMPKIN also known as squash; a vegetable with golden flesh. Any type of pumpkin or butternut squash can be used.

RHUBARB a vegetable with pinkish stalks, which are generally cooked and eaten as a fruit.

RIND also known as zest; the outer layer of all citrus fruits.

RUM, DARK we used an underproof (not overproof) rum.

SAMBAL OELEK (also ulek or olek) Indonesian in origin, a salty paste made from ground chillies, vinegar and various spices.

SEMOLINA coarsely milled inner part of wheat grains.

SUGAR we used coarse granulated table sugar, also known as crystal sugar, unless otherwise specified.

brown a soft, fine granulated sugar containing molasses.

caster also known as superfine; a fine granulated table sugar.

demerara golden crystal sugar.

icing also known as confectioners' sugar or powdered sugar.

raw natural brown granulated sugar.

SULTANAS also known as golden raisins; dried, seedless, white grapes.

YEAST allow 2 teaspoons (7g) dried yeast to each 15g compressed yeast if substituting one for the other; see also page 37 of this book for helpful information.

index

conversion charts

MEASURES

■ The spoon measurements used in this book are metric: one metric tablespoon holds 20ml; one metric teaspoon holds 5ml.

■ All spoon measurements are level.

■ The most accurate way of measuring dry ingredients is to weigh them.

■ When measuring liquids, use a clear glass or plastic jug with metric markings.

■ We use large eggs with an average weight of 60g.

DRY MEASURES

metric	imperial
15g	$^1/_2$oz
30g	1oz
60g	2oz
90g	3oz
125g	4oz ($^1/_4$lb)
155g	5oz
185g	6oz
220g	7oz
250g	8oz ($^1/_2$lb)
280g	9oz
315g	10oz
345g	11oz
375g	12oz ($^3/_4$lb)
410g	13oz
440g	14oz
470g	15oz
500g	16oz (1lb)
750g	24oz (1$^1/_2$lb)
1kg	32oz (2lb)

LIQUID MEASURES

metric	imperial
30ml	1 fl oz
60ml	2 fl oz
100ml	3 fl oz
125ml	4 fl oz
150ml	5 fl oz ($^1/_4$ pint/1 gill)
190ml	6 fl oz
250ml	8 fl oz
300ml	10 fl oz ($^1/_2$ pt)
500ml	16 fl oz
600ml	20 fl oz (1 pint)
1000ml (1 litre)	1$^3/_4$ pints

LENGTH MEASURES

metric	imperial
3mm	$^1/_8$in
6mm	$^1/_4$in
1cm	$^1/_2$in
2cm	$^3/_4$in
2.5cm	1in
5cm	2in
6cm	2$^1/_2$in
8cm	3in
10cm	4in
13cm	5in
15cm	6in
18cm	7in
20cm	8in
23cm	9in
25cm	10in
28cm	11in
30cm	12in (1ft)

OVEN TEMPERATURES

These oven temperatures are only a guide for conventional ovens. For fan-assisted ovens, check the manufacturer's manual.

	°C (Celcius)	°F (Fahrenheit)	gas mark
Very low	120	250	$^1/_2$
Low	150	275-300	1-2
Moderately low	170	325	3
Moderate	180	350-375	4-5
Moderately hot	200	400	6
Hot	220	425-450	7-8
Very hot	240	475	9